WILD ABOUT ANIMALS

HEDGEHOGS

By Emma Huddleston

Kaleidoscope
Minneapolis, MN

The Quest for Discovery Never Ends

This edition first published in 2020 by Kaleidoscope Publishing, Inc.

For information regarding permission, write to
Kaleidoscope Publishing, Inc.
6012 Blue Circle Drive
Minnetonka, MN 55343

Library of Congress Control Number
2019938853

ISBN
978-1-64519-007-3 (library bound)
978-1-64494-249-9 (paperback)
978-1-64519-107-0 (ebook)

Printed in the United States of America.

Bigfoot lurks within one of the images in this book. It's up to you to find him!

TABLE OF CONTENTS

CHAPTER 1

Quills

Leaves rustle. Twigs snap. A small animal crawls out of a bush. It's a hedgehog. He has leaves stuck to his back. He shakes a little bit. One falls off. Hedgehogs are **mammals**. Most mammals have soft fur or hair. But not him. He has a thick layer of spikes on his back called quills. They fall out and grow back like hair.

FUN FACT

Quills are made of keratin, just like human hair and fingernails are.

Hedgehogs are found around the world.

PARTS OF A HEDGEHOG

The hedgehog is light brown. His coat has bands of different colors along the quills. Some are brown and black. They help him blend into bushes and leaves. His belly and face are covered in thick hair. They don't have quills. His body is 12 inches (30 cm) long. He is fully grown. He weighs 2.4 pounds (1.1 kg). He is bigger than most hedgehogs.

A hedgehog's coat lets the mammal blend into its surroundings.

The hedgehog wanders into a garden. He looks for food in the hedge. He digs into roots and bushes. Where he finds food is part of how he got his name. He eats mostly insects. He also eats worms, centipedes, and snails. Sometimes he finds fruits, leaves, grasses, or seeds. It depends on what is near. He snorts and grunts while he eats. His noises sound like a pig. That is how he got the name hedgehog.

GARDEN FRIENDS

Some people like hedgehogs in their garden. Hedgehogs eat garden pests. This keeps flower beds and vegetable gardens healthy. Some people in Europe make nests of straw or hay for hedgehogs.

Hedgehogs eat common pests. This helps protect gardens.

CHAPTER 2

Small but Mighty

A hedgehog sniffs the ground. She has weak eyes. That means she must use other senses to find food. She uses her nose and ears. Her ears are big compared to her body. Her long **snout** is wet. It smells food. She pokes it into the dirt to find a worm.

FUN FACT

Hedgehogs have 3,000 to 5,000 quills covering their body.

Her legs are strong. She has big feet with five toes. Curved claws make her a good digger. She finds the worm. Yum! She eats it. She has up to forty-four teeth for chewing. Then she hears another insect. She crawls along the bush. Hedgehogs can travel up to 2 miles (3 km) a day. They look for food and find places to rest.

Hedgehogs have a great sense of smell.

She eats in the dark. Hedgehogs are **nocturnal**. Most **predators** are awake during the day. So in the day, she hides and sleeps. She curls into a ball. This position protects her. Her spiky quills are facing out. Predators won't want to eat her. She can sleep for up to eighteen hours.

HOW BIG ARE HEDGEHOGS?

Hedgehogs can be 4 TO 12 INCHES (10 TO 30 CM) long, depending on the type!

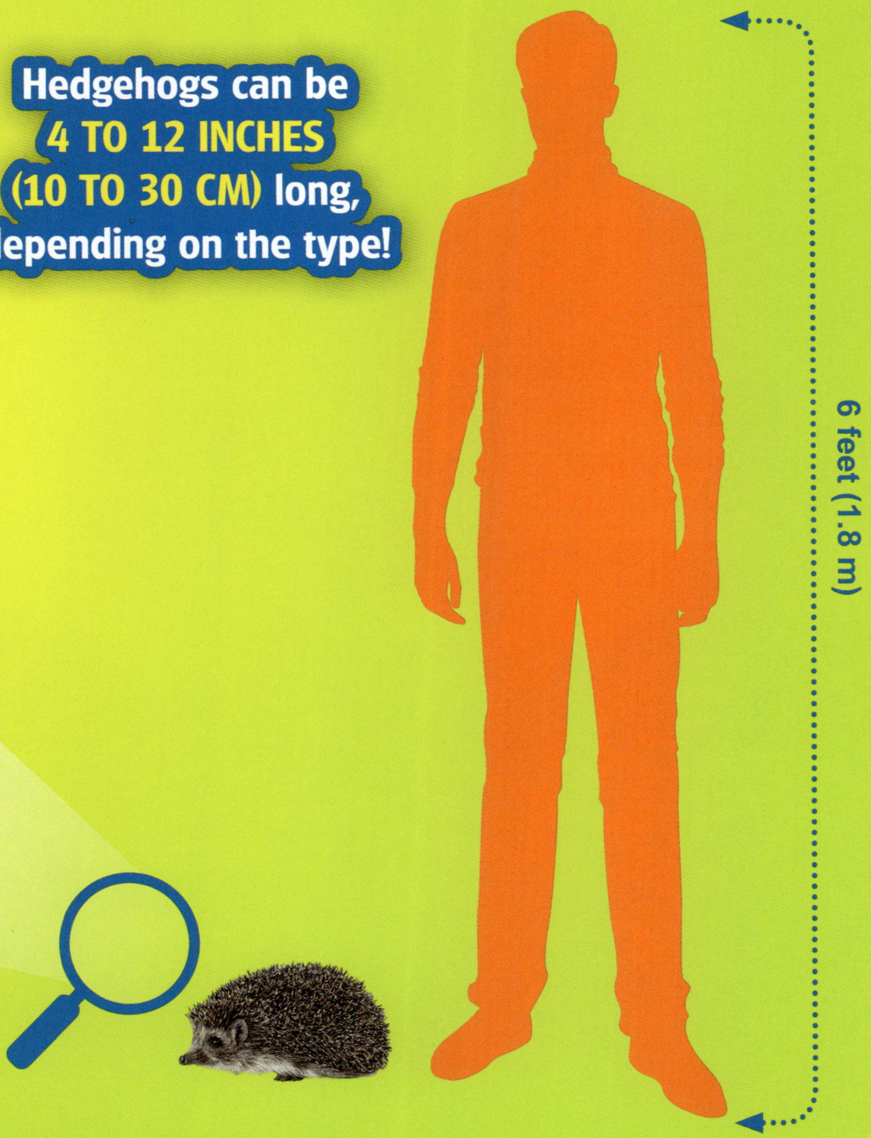

Hedgehogs can curl into a ball to protect themselves.

An owl spots the hedgehog below. The hedgehog tucks into a ball. Extra skin on her body stretches. She uses the muscles on her belly and back. Her soft belly is protected. Her quills raise into a crisscross pattern. They are her best defense. Quills are stiff and sharp like body armor. The ball is difficult for predators to pull open. The owl flies away. The hedgehog is safe.

MYTHS

Many people think hedgehogs are related to porcupines. Both animals have quills, but they are not closely related. Some people think hedgehogs can roll when they are curled into a ball. They cannot. Also, hedgehogs cannot shoot quills. Quills are like hairs on a human head. They break, fall out, and regrow.

CHAPTER 3

Living in Burrows

A hedgehog digs into the dirt. He makes a **burrow** 20 inches (50 cm) deep. The burrow keeps him safe during the day while he sleeps. Some hedgehogs use holes left by turtles, foxes, or other animals.

FUN FACT

Hedgehogs only weigh 0.3 to 3.5 pounds (0.1 to 1.6 kg), depending on the species.

A hedgehog in the desert crawls into a burrow. She is protected from the heat. A hedgehog in the forest gathers dead leaves, twigs, and grass. He adds them to his burrow to make it blend in with the surroundings. It will be harder for predators to see the burrow. Hedgehog **habitats** are diverse. Hedgehogs can live in deserts or woodlands. They live around the world. They are naturally found in Europe, Asia, and Africa. There are seventeen different **species** of hedgehogs.

Hedgehogs live in many different habitats.

Where Do Hedgehogs Live?

A female hedgehog comes out of the tall grass. It is late at night. Water droplets cover the grass. It's springtime. She sees a male hedgehog nearby. She sniffs his body and follows him. Hedgehogs live alone most of their life. They only come together to mate.

She gives birth after several weeks. A **litter** can have up to eleven babies. Baby hedgehogs are called hoglets. Their quills are covered in pink skin at first. The mother licks one of the hoglets. After his first day, 150 white quills poke through. His skin shrinks.

Hoglets' quills grow in before their hair.

He is strong after one week. He pushes one of the other hoglets over to get milk from his mother's body. He is hungry. The hoglet stays with his mother for several weeks. She protects him. He grows. The quills on his back get darker. They become pointy and strong. When he is several weeks old, he leaves. He lives on his own. Hedgehogs can live three to eight years in the wild and up to ten years in zoos.

Hedgehogs live on their own.

HEDGEHOG SOUNDS

Hedgehogs huff and puff when they are content. The noises are natural. They make them while walking and digging. Hedgehogs make a different sound when they are unhappy. They hiss and click.

CHAPTER 4

Protecting Hedgehogs

Leo lives in Texas. He has a pet hedgehog. She is not easy to care for. Leo bought her a warm cage and a wheel. She runs on the wheel to let out her energy. But her wheel is messy. He cleans it every three days. She poops and pees while she runs. It gets all over her feet and belly. Leo thinks the hardest part is that she is nocturnal. He hears her running and eating at night. Sometimes it keeps him awake.

Hedgehogs can be difficult to care for.

Some people own hedgehogs as pets. Others worry this hurts hedgehogs.

Hedgehogs are most active at night.

Bella loves hedgehogs. She saw one taking a bath in a video online. It was cute. Now she wants to have a pet hedgehog. But she lives in Georgia. It is illegal to have them as pets in Georgia and some other US states. Hedgehogs can carry illnesses. They are not native to North America. This means they could harm other animals or insects if they are let into the wild. Some people worry about hedgehogs as pets. Their owners wake them up during the day to play. Hedgehogs in the wild sleep at that time.

FUN FACT

Hedgehogs can move at speeds up to 6.5 feet (2 m) per second.

Hugh's garden in England used to have many hedgehogs. He would see more than one every week. Today, he hopes to see a hedgehog. But their populations are going down. In the 1950s, more than 36 million hedgehogs lived in the United Kingdom. In 2013, fewer than 1 million were left. The biggest threat to hedgehogs is habitat loss. Hedgehogs have fewer places to live because of humans.

Hugh saw cities in England expand. New roads and offices were built. They cut through gardens and parks. In China, Mongolia, and Russia, some farmers use poison to kill small animals. Farms in India and Pakistan expand into desert land where hedgehogs live. Hedgehog populations are going down slowly around the world. Hugh wants to protect hedgehogs for the future. Learning more about hedgehogs helps people protect them.

Hedgehogs are threatened by habitat loss.

BEYOND THE BOOK

After reading the book, it's time to think about what you learned. Try the following exercises to jumpstart your ideas.

THINK

DIFFERENT SOURCES. Think about what types of sources you could find on hedgehogs. What could you find in an encyclopedia? What could you learn at a museum? What about an interview with a zookeeper? How could each of the sources be useful in its own way?

CREATE

SHARPEN YOUR RESEARCH SKILLS. Hedgehogs live in habitats around the world. Where could you go in the library to find more information about hedgehogs' habitats? Who could you talk to who might know more? Create a research plan. Write a paragraph about your next steps.

SHARE

WHAT'S YOUR OPINION? People have different opinions about whether hedgehogs should be allowed as pets. Some people think it is harmful to the owner and the hedgehog. Do you agree or disagree with this position? Use evidence from the text to support your answer. Share your position and evidence with a friend. Does your friend agree with you?

GROW

REAL-LIFE RESEARCH. What places could you visit to learn more about hedgehogs? What other things could you learn while you were there?

RESEARCH NINJA

Visit www.ninjaresearcher.com/0073 to learn how to take your research skills and book report writing to the next level!

RESEARCH

DIGITAL LITERACY TOOLS

SEARCH LIKE A PRO

Learn about how to use search engines to find useful websites.

FACT OR FAKE?

Discover how you can tell a trusted website from an untrustworthy resource.

TEXT DETECTIVE

Explore how to zero in on the information you need most.

SHOW YOUR WORK

Research responsibly—learn how to cite sources.

WRITE

GET TO THE POINT

Learn how to express your main ideas.

PLAN OF ATTACK

Learn prewriting exercises and create an outline.

DOWNLOADABLE REPORT FORMS

Further Resources

BOOKS

Doudna, Kelly. *Hilarious Hedgehogs*. Abdo Publishing, 2013.

Mattern, Joanne. *Porcupines and Hedgehogs*. Red Chair Press, 2017.

Schuetz, Kari. *Mammals*. Bellwether Media, 2013.

WEBSITES

FACTSURFER

Factsurfer.com gives you a safe, fun way to find more information.

1. Go to www.factsurfer.com.
2. Enter "Hedgehogs" into the search box and click 🔍.
3. Select your book cover to see a list of related websites.

Glossary

burrow: A burrow is a hole in the ground made by an animal for shelter. The hedgehog made a burrow to hide from predators.

habitats: Habitats are places where animals live. Hedgehogs are found in habitats around the world.

litter: A litter is a group of babies born at the same time. A litter of hedgehogs can have eleven babies.

mammals: Animals that are mammals give birth, drink milk from their mother, and have hair. Hedgehogs are mammals.

nocturnal: A nocturnal animal sleeps during the day and is active at night. Hedgehogs are nocturnal, which makes them difficult pets.

pests: Pests are insects that are annoying to humans. Hedgehogs eat garden pests.

predators: Predators are animals that hunt and eat other animals. Hedgehogs roll into a ball to protect themselves from predators.

snout: A snout is a long nose. Hedgehogs use their snout to hunt in the dirt for worms.

species: Animals that are the same species can breed together and have offspring. There are seventeen species of hedgehogs.

Index

PHOTO CREDITS

The images in this book are reproduced through the courtesy of: Ondrej Prosicky/Shutterstock Images, front cover; Viorel Sima/Shutterstock Images, p. 3; Eric Isselee/Shutterstock Images, p. 4; Coatesy/Shutterstock Images, pp. 4–5, 7, 8, 9, 14–15, 16–17, 27; DioGen/Shutterstock Images, pp. 6, 12, 13 (hedgehog); Henderbeth/Shutterstock Images, pp. 10–11; Chipmunk131/Shutterstock Images, p. 13 (person); Robert Eastman/Shutterstock Images, p. 15; Red Line Editorial, p. 18; thanapol thanalad/Shutterstock Images, p. 19; Alena Sekerakova/Shutterstock Images, p. 20; nomad-photo.eu/Shutterstock Images, pp. 20–21; Andrii Butko84/Shutterstock Images, p. 22; Kuttelvaserova Stuchelova/Shutterstock Images, p. 23; pics of my life/Shutterstock Images, pp. 24–25; Phonix_a Pk.sarote/Shutterstock Images, pp. 26–27; skydie/Shutterstock Images, p. 30.

ABOUT THE AUTHOR

Emma Huddleston has written books about science, sports, animals, and more. She thinks animals are fascinating. When she isn't writing, she enjoys reading and swing dancing. She lives in the Twin Cities with her husband.